IES   F48230   11-7-03

The Life of Plants

Plant Parts

Richard & Louise Spilsbury

Heinemann LIBRARY

H **www.heinemann.co.uk**
Visit our website to find out more information about **Heinemann Library** books.

To order:
☎ Phone 44 (0) 1865 888066
🖹 Send a fax to 44 (0) 1865 314091
🖥 Visit the Heinemann Bookshop at www.heinemann.co.uk to browse our catalogue and order online.

First published in Great Britain by Heinemann Library,
Halley Court, Jordan Hill, Oxford OX2 8EJ
a division of Harcourt Education
Heinemann is a registered trademark of Harcourt Education Ltd.

© Harcourt Education Ltd 2002

Designed by Macwiz
Illustrated by Jeff Edwards
Originated by Ambassador Litho Ltd
Printed by Wing King Tong, Hong Kong

ISBN 0 431 11880 9
06 05 04 03 02
10 9 8 7 6 5 4 3 2 1

British Library Cataloguing in Publication Data
Spilsbury, Louise
    Plant parts. - (Life of plants)
    1. Plant physiology - Juvenile literature
    I. Title II. Spilsbury, Richard, 1963-
    571.2

Acknowledgements
The Publishers would like to thank the following for permission to reproduce photographs:
Bruce Coleman: p15; Corbis: pp27, 37; FLPA: pp13, 21; Garden matters: p17; Holt Studios: pp5, 7, 8, 9, 10, 11, 12, 14, 16, 18, 22, 25, 28, 29, 31, 35, 38; Oxford Scientific Films: pp4, 26, 32, 33, 39; Science Photo Library: pp24, 34, Andrew Syred p30, Claude Nurisany and Marie Perennou p19, Will and Deni McIntyre p36

Cover photograph reproduced with permission of Tudor Photography.

Our thanks to Andrew Solway for his comments in the preparation of this book.

Every effort has been made to contact copyright holders of any material reproduced in this book. Any omissions will be rectified in subsequent printings if notice is given to the Publisher.

Contents

Any words appearing in the text in bold, **like this**, are explained in the glossary.

A plant may be called different things in different countries, so every type of plant has a Latin name that can be recognized anywhere in the world. Latin names are made of two words – the first is the genus (general group) a plant belongs to and the second is its species (specific) name. Latin plant names are given in brackets throughout this book.

Looking at plants

There is a bewildering variety of plants in the world. They range from tiny, barely visible plants that you might step on without noticing as you walk on a mountain, to huge cacti in a hot, sandy desert. Yet even though plants all over the world look so incredibly different, most of them are made up of the same basic parts.

Plants all over

Scientists estimate that there are more than 300,000 **species** of plants in the world, of which around 260,000 are flowering plants. However, no one knows for sure. It is likely that there are even more species of plants out there that have not yet been discovered.

▲ All flowering plants – the most common kind of plants – have parts called **roots, stems, leaves** and **flowers**. On some plants, flowers are massive; on others – like this wood anemone, they are small. Some plants have thin, floppy stems, like this, while others have stems as hard as iron.

◄ Different plant parts all have a particular job to do, even though they may look very different on each kind of plant.

A job to do

Each part of a plant has a job to do. Plants, like other **organisms**, need food to live, grow and repair themselves. Animals eat plants, or they eat other animals that eat plants. Plants make their own food by a special process called **photosynthesis**, using sunlight, water and **carbon dioxide**. Some parts of the plant collect these ingredients and other parts put them together to make food.

Like other organisms, plants also need to **reproduce**. They reproduce so that their species can survive after their death. Plants have special parts that allow them to reproduce, when the time is right.

In this book we will be looking at the different parts that grow on many of the plants across the world. We will discover many of the different forms these parts can take and the clever things they do.

Plant building blocks

All organisms are made up of tiny living parts called **cells**. They are so small you can usually only see them using a microscope. Not all plant cells are the same. Different groups of cells form different plant parts and they help that part do its job. Most plant cells look like minuscule, water-filled balloons, with a tiny, rigid cell wall. Plant cells have these walls; animal cells do not.

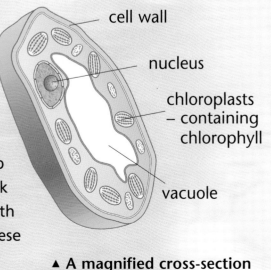

cell wall

nucleus

chloroplasts – containing chlorophyll

vacuole

▲ A magnified cross-section of a typical plant cell.

Leaves

Leaves come in many different sizes, shapes and arrangements. Leaf shapes are one of the clues that can tell you what kind of plant you are looking at. For example, the leaves of the banana plant are flat, wide and can be several metres long. The leaves of the aloe are thick with tough skins but jelly-like insides.

Leaves can be oval, circular, star-shaped or heart-shaped. Some leaves, such as spinach, have smooth, rounded edges, but others, such as sweet chestnut (*Castanea sativa*), have jagged edges. Most leaves are made up of one piece, like the maple (*Acer*). Others, however, such as those on the ash (*Fraxinus*), are made up of smaller leaves, called 'leaflets', all joined to a central **stalk**.

World's longest leaves

The raffia palm (*Raphia farinifera*) has the longest leaves of all palm trees. Its leaves grow up to 20 metres long – which is about the same as two coaches parked end to end!

◄▲ These photos give you an idea of the huge variety of leaf shapes, sizes and colours there are on plants around the world.

Leaf structure

Even though leaves look very different, they usually have the same parts. The flat bit of a leaf is called the **blade**. Leaf blades grow from the **stem** on a stalk, although some grow straight out of the stem. The leaf stalk (called the **petiole**) can bend so that the leaf does not snap off the plant if it is hit by a gust of wind.

The petiole is attached to a **midrib**, which runs along the centre of the leaf blade. On plants such as the beech (*Fagus*), leaf **veins** branch off from this central midrib. On other plants, such as buffalo grass (*Buchloe dactyloides*), the leaf veins are all lined up from bottom to top. The veins form a network of tubes that connect the leaf to all the other parts of the plant. Water taken in by the **roots** of the plant moves to the leaves through these tubes, and sugary liquid (**sap**), which carries food from the leaves to other parts of the plant, also travels through them.

▼ Different plants have leaves with different vein patterns. If you hold a vine leaf, like this one, up to the light, you should be able to see the network of veins that run through it.

The veins act a bit like the bones in our bodies. They help keep the leaf blade stiff and flat. If you see a dead leaf rotting under a tree or bush you can see the leaf skeleton (network of veins) very easily. The leaf skeleton takes longer to rot than the leaf blade because it is made of tougher **cells**.

blade

vein

midrib

stalk (petiole)

Looking at leaves

Leaves are one of the most important parts of any plant. Leaves help plants get the sunlight and **carbon dioxide** that they need to make their own food, which they do in a process called **photosynthesis**. In photosynthesis, plants use the **energy** from sunlight to combine the carbon dioxide and water, turning them into energy-rich foods, such as sugars.

To get light, many leaves are large and flat because that is the best shape for absorbing (soaking up) lots of light. Bigger plants need more food to keep them going than smaller plants, so they often have several big leaves or thousands of small ones in order to make enough.

◄ The leaves on this banana fan palm are arranged so that they don't overlap each other. That way each leaf gets as much light as it can.

Light-catching leaves

Have you ever wondered why leaves grow where they do on plants? They are often positioned high up on a **stem** to receive as much light as possible. Stems and **stalks** hold the leaves out so they can get a share of the light. Sometimes leaves grow alternately – first one side of the stem and then the other, a bit further up. Some grow in a spiral around the stem or opposite each other, in pairs from the same point on the stem.

Close up!

Take a good, close look at a leaf. The upper side of the leaf is different from the underside. It often has a waxier, thicker surface than the underside. Most photosynthesis happens in the **cells** of the leaf's upper side, so this is the side that always faces the sun. Warmth from the sun **evaporates** water inside the leaf, so the waxy coat reduces the amount of water the leaf loses.

On the underside of a leaf there are lots of little holes called **stomata**. These are so small that there may be thousands of stomata in every square centimetre of the leaf's surface. The plant opens its stomata to take in the air it needs for photosynthesis. It can also close them when it is hot, to stop too much water evaporating.

Why are leaves green?

Most leaves are green. This is because they contain a green substance called **chlorophyll**. Chlorophyll is essential for photosynthesis. The leaves of some plants are different colours, such as reddish purple in copper beech (*Fagus purpurea*). Their leaves still contain chlorophyll, but another pigment, the red colour, is stronger.

▼ All plants need water to live. The stomata holes that control the amount of water that plants lose from their leaves can only be seen through a microscope.

Needles and spines

Some people find it hard to believe that the long, thin needles of a pine tree and the sharp spines of a cactus plant are really kinds of **leaves**. They *are* leaves and they grow in these special shapes to help the plants they grow on to survive.

Pine trees are **coniferous**. They are able to survive cold weather, when water in the ground may be locked up in ice, because of the form of their leaves. If you look closely at pine needles you will see they have a groove on the underside. The leaf's **stomata** are inside the groove. This shelters them from wintry winds that might **evaporate** water from inside the leaf. A thick, waxy coating on the needles gives them extra protection.

Most cacti live in hot, dry deserts. Cactus spines are very thin leaves. Like needles, they lose very little water by evaporation. Unlike conifers, which carry out **photosynthesis** in their green needles, cacti plants make their food in their thick **stems**. The spines that come straight out of the stem are often brown. The stems are green, because they contain the **chlorophyll** necessary for photosynthesis.

▼ Cactus spines have many uses! The sharp spines on this cactus also help to defend it from animals that want to eat the watery flesh inside its stem.

Kinds of needles

Some needles, such as white cedar (*Thuja occidentalis*), are short, soft and flat like scales. Other needles, such as Eastern white pine (*Pinus strobus*), are around 10 centimetres long and grow in groups of five. Juniper (*Juniperus*) needles grow in groups of three. The leaves of the monkey-puzzle tree (*Araucaria araucana*) are tough and triangular, and grow in spirals along its branches. They are very sharp to protect its **cones** from being eaten by animals.

▲ The needles of a conifer tree.

Deciduous and coniferous leaves

The broad, flat leaves of **deciduous** trees such as common beech (*Fagus sylvatica*), would be damaged by cold winter weather. So they shed (drop) their leaves in autumn and grow new ones in the spring, when the weather is warmer. In winter, their branches are bare.

Coniferous trees, such as the Scots pine in the picture, are those that have cones and needle-like leaves, such as common spruce (*Picea abies*) or Douglas fir (*Pseudotsuga menziesii*). Their tough, thick and waxy leaves can survive harsh winter weather. Such trees do not need to shed all their leaves in autumn; they drop some old leaves and grow some new leaves throughout the year. Some people call such trees evergreens, because they always look green.

Buds

When new **leaves** suddenly appear on trees in spring on a **deciduous** tree, where do they come from? The answer is from tiny packages called **buds**. If you look at a tree in winter, the buds are already there, at the ends and along the lengths of the twigs and branches.

A deciduous tree stops or slows down growth in winter, but its buds are ready to quickly start growing again in spring. Inside the buds, tiny leaves wait, folded neatly in their protective case. When warmth and light from spring sunshine hits the buds, they begin to grow and swell until they burst open and the leaves emerge. Once the leaves are out, they can start to make food for the tree.

Different buds

Different plants have different kinds of buds. The horse chestnut tree (*Aesculus hippocastanum*) has large, sticky buds. The ash tree (*Fraxinus excelsior*) has small buds that are as black as ash from a dead fire. The buds of the lily-flowered magnolia tree (*Magnolia liliiflora*) are covered in soft, thick fur. In winter, when there are no leaves to help you identify a tree, a good look at the buds can help you work out what it is.

◄ **The buds on a horse chestnut tree are sticky to put off insects that might try to eat them.**

Flower buds

Flowers can seem to appear on a plant as if by magic. One day they are not there; the next they are. Flowers are able to appear so swiftly, when the conditions are right, because they are already formed, in miniature, inside buds. Covers called **sepals** protect the fragile, folded young flower **petals** just inside the bud. After the sepals have opened, the petals grow and spread out of a flower bud rapidly. Some kinds of plants, such as tulips, produce only one flower, so they will grow only one bud. Others, like apple trees, grow many flowers, which burst out of many small and tightly packed buds.

Hibernating plants?

Most of us have heard of bears hibernating – but plants? **Bulbs** are like underground buds and they allow certain plants to rest through winter when the cold weather could kill them. Onions are a well-known kind of bulb. Bulbs consist of layers of thick, fleshy leaves surrounding a central bud. A papery skin protects the whole bulb. In autumn the plant parts above ground die. The bulb survives the winter underground, waiting to grow new leaves and flowers from its bud in the warmth of the following spring.

▲ Tulip flowers bursting out of their buds. First the bud swells and grows. Then the petals push their way out of the sepals into the light.

Flowers

There is an immense variety of **flowers** in the world. Single flowers range in size from just a few millimetres to a metre across. Some are simple in shape and pattern, while others are incredibly complicated. Flowers may be blue, yellow, white, red or purple, or a combination of colours. Flowers across the world may all look very different, but the basic parts of a flower are the same.

Flowers grow out of **buds**. The swollen end of the flower nearest the **stem** is called a **receptacle**. The other parts of the flower are above this. On the outside are the **sepals**, which protect the young, fragile flower parts as they develop. They often look like small green **leaves**. **Petals** are usually the largest and most colourful part of a flower.

anther

carpel

ovary

stamen

▲ **This photo of a tulip shows the different parts in its flower.**

The reproductive parts

A flower is the headquarters of the plant's **reproductive** system – it is where the **seeds**, which may grow into new plants, are made. A flower contains male and female parts. The female parts are called the **carpel**. At the bottom is the **ovary**, which produces and holds the female **sex cells**. The **stamens** are the male parts. The **anthers**, at the top of each stamen, produce male sex cells, each of which is stored inside a protective **pollen** grain.

How do flowers work?

In order to produce a seed, a male sex cell must fuse (join) with a female sex cell from the same plant or a different plant of the same **species**. This is called **fertilization**. To do this, pollen must move from an anther to an ovary. This movement is called **pollination**, and it often happens with the help of insects. This is where the flower's petals and **nectary** come in useful. A nectary is a small sac at the bottom of a petal that contains sweet liquid called **nectar**. Insects visit flowers to feed on the nectar. Pollen from the anthers brushes onto their bodies. When they stop off at another flower, it rubs off again, hopefully onto the top of a carpel.

▲ Insects are attracted to flowers by their colourful petals and sweet scent.

When the pollen grain lands at the top of a carpel, the male sex cell inside moves down into the ovary. It joins with the female cells and a seed starts to grow.

Awesome flowers

The largest single flower in the world is the rafflesia (see right). Once every ten years it produces a foul-smelling flower that grows up to a metre wide and 7 kilograms in weight. However, the titan arum is possibly even more spectacular. It produces a tower of tiny flowers, which can be 3 metres high!

15

Kinds of flowers

Different **species** of plants have different colours, shapes and arrangements of **flowers**. Bluebells (*Scilla*) have **petals** that are joined together to form a bell. Violets (*Viola*) have petals of different shapes all on one flower. In clematis flowers, it is the **sepals** that are colourful, not the petals. In fuchsias, both the sepals and petals are brightly coloured as a kind of double act to draw insects' attention to them. Sometimes the sepals and petals look exactly the same. This is common in lilies, for example.

In some flowers, such as sunflowers, dandelions and daisies, the 'petals' are not petals at all – each is part of a tiny flower called a floret. In sunflowers the centre of the flower is made up of florets too. The whole flower-like head (called an **inflorescence**) contains hundreds of separate flowers! Each floret is a flower in its own right because each is capable of making a **seed**.

Flower tricks

Try this trick on your friends. Hold a daisy in your hand and ask them how many flowers you are holding. When they say one, you can surprise them with the fact that actually there are about 250. Pull a daisy to bits and you will see that the daisy is not one flower, but many tiny flowers (florets) joined together. The yellow central part of the daisy is made up of many tiny, tube-shaped florets. On the edge of the daisy there are different florets, each with a pink petal on it.

Flower forms

Each species of plant always grows its flowers in a particular way. The way flowers are arranged on a plant is as important for identifying them as the colour or size of their petals.

Some plants, like the tulip or crocus, grow a single flower out of the end of a single **stem**. Others, like scabious (*Scabiosa*), grow lots of flowers, each one developing and opening, often at different times and on different stems. The flowers of some plants grow in spires or spikes. Foxglove (*Digitalis purpurea*) flowers grow on little **stalks** coming out of the stem. The flowers at the bottom usually look bigger than the ones at the top because they open first.

▲ The umbrella-like shape of an umbellifer, like giant hogweed, provides a helpful platform for insects to land on.

Other plants have flowers that grow in groups called **clusters**. Some have lots of small flowers on separate little stalks growing out of the top of the stem. Sometimes these flowers droop down, as in giant yellow cowslips (*Primula florindae*). In some plants, such as giant hogweed (*Heracleum*), many flowers all grow from the same point on the stalk. If the tiny flowers are raised up until they are almost at the same level together, they look a bit like an umbrella. In fact, the name for this shape of flower is an **umbel**.

What is a fruit?

If someone asked you to name three fruits, the chances are you would come up with suggestions like oranges, bananas, apples or pears. But would you think of the 'helicopters' (keys) on a sycamore or maple tree, or pea **pods** or cucumber? In science, the word 'fruit' means the part of a flowering plant in which **seeds** develop.

Fruits of different **species** can look very different, but they all share two important jobs – to protect developing seeds and to help move them away from the plant. Seeds start to develop if **pollination** has happened. When a plant has finished flowering, the **petals** on its **flowers** die and fall off the plant. The hollow part at the bottom of the flower, called the **ovary**, starts to swell. This is usually the part that slowly grows into a fruit.

◀ After a tomato flower's petals fall from the plant, its ovary swells into a round green fruit. The tomato turns red when the seeds inside are ready.

Apples are not fruits!

The true fruit of an apple tree is the core, as this is the ovary that holds the seeds. The fleshy part of the apple – the bit we eat and think of as the fruit – is actually the swollen top of the flower stalk (the **receptacle**). The fleshy part has grown around the real fruit. Other 'false fruits' like this include pears and rosehips.

Kinds of fruits

Some fruits are fleshy (soft and juicy). Fleshy fruits such as cherries or apricots have only one seed inside them, contained in a hard 'stone'. Other fleshy fruits, such as melon, cucumber or tomato, have lots of seeds, scattered throughout the flesh or in a central core. Blackberries and loganberries are compound fruits. Each seed is contained in its own parcel of sweet flesh, and lots of parcels together form the compound fruit. Some plants, such as pumpkins, produce a few giant fruits. Others, like elder, produce hundreds of small fruits called berries.

Dry fruits include the pods of soya beans, the seed capsules of poppies, and the winged seed cases of plane trees (*Platanus*). The dry fruit of the horse chestnut is hard and spiky to protect the seed inside from being eaten before it drops to the ground.

◄ The dry poppy fruit is like a pepper pot. As the wind blows, the seeds are shaken out from holes in the top.

Fruit without seeds

Sometimes you open a fruit such as a grape or banana and find no seeds. Plants are rarely like this in the wild – a fruit's most important job is to look after its seeds. But many people don't like to eat fruit that has seeds, so fruit growers develop varieties without seeds.

Why do plants have fruits?

One of the things a new young plant needs to grow well is space. It needs room to spread its **roots** and unfold its **leaves** into the light. If a seedling (young plant) tries to grow when it is too close to other plants, including its parent plant, it will have to compete for the things it needs. Plants cannot move, so how do they ensure that the **seeds** they produce end up somewhere new? The answer is **fruit**! Fruits protect the developing seeds but also use clever ways to disperse (scatter) them.

Fruits come in different shapes, sizes and forms depending on the way they spread their seeds. Some plants use the wind, water or animals to help disperse their seeds. Others have fruits that suddenly split or pop open, catapulting seeds away from the plant.

▲ The dry fruits of the maple tree have two light, spreading wings. When they fall from the tree their shape helps them to fall and spin in the air, carrying the seeds away from their parent plant.

Fruits that are dispersed by the wind, water or explosion are usually light and fairly small, like poppy seeds. Maple keys have wings so that they can spin away from their parent tree. Dandelion fruits have hairs that act like miniature parachutes when caught by the wind, taking them long distances in the air.

Some fruits, such as those of the alder tree, are dispersed by water. Alder trees grow by rivers so their fruits drop into the water. Oil in the case around the alder seed helps it float until it lands somewhere that it might grow.

Plants that use explosion to disperse their seeds have specially shaped fruits. Peapods twist and dry up when their seeds are fully developed. The twisting makes the two halves of the **pods** burst open, scattering the seeds around.

Animal assistance

The skins of many fruits are colourful and appealing, and the flesh is sweet and good to eat. This is no accident. When a bird or other animal is attracted to eat a fruit it often swallows it whole – skin, flesh and seeds. Later on, the seeds fall to the ground in the animal's droppings. Such seeds usually have extra-tough outer cases so they are not damaged as they pass through the animal's gut. Animals also spit out seeds or drop partly eaten fruit far away from the plant on which the fruit grew.

▲ Orangutans love to eat durians. The strong smell helps to direct them to the trees where the fruit grow.

The forbidden fruit

Durian is a type of spiky fruit weighing several kilograms that grows in South-east Asia. The skin of durian has a disgusting smell (like rotting fish) but its custard-like flesh is delicious to eat. In Singapore, people are not allowed to take durians on many taxis, buses and aeroplanes because the smell is so unpleasant to most people!

Seeds

All flowering plants make **seeds**. Seeds come in a huge variety of sizes, shapes and colours. Some seeds are so small they look like dust or grains of powder. The seeds of some **rainforest** orchids are so tiny that millions of their seeds would weigh less than 1 gram. At the other end of the scale, an individual seed on a coconut tree usually weighs more than 2 kilograms.

Seeds are like parcels with tiny plants inside. Each seed contains what it needs to start growing into a new plant. Inside a seed there is an **embryo** (a partly developed plant or seedling) and a store of plant food. This food is used to keep the embryo alive while it is inside the seed, and to give it **energy** to **germinate**. Most seeds also need water, air and the right temperature to germinate.

Most seeds store their food in special tiny **seed leaves**. The seed leaves also form the first **leaves** that emerge from the seed once it germinates. Some plants, such as maize, have only one seed leaf in their seeds. Others, such as broad beans, have two.

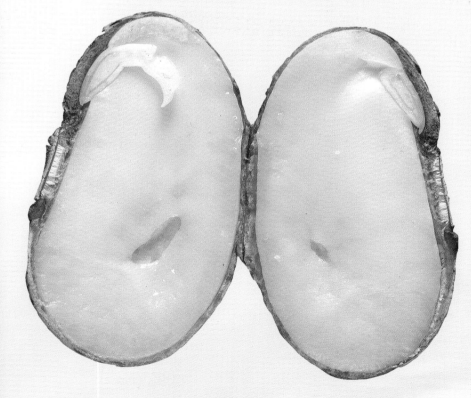

◄ Seeds are like little parcels. The seed coat keeps the embryo and seed leaves safe until the conditions are right for it to start to grow into a new plant.

Seed coats

The outer layer of a seed is called the seed coat. It does three important jobs. It protects the embryo from injury, perhaps when the seed drops from the plant. It also protects the food supply, stopping the food-rich seed leaves inside from being eaten by insects and other animals. The seed coat also stops the seed from losing water and so prevents it from drying out completely.

Seeds and germination

Having an efficient seed coat is important because most seeds remain **dormant** instead of germinating straight after they leave the parent plant. This rest period stops seeds from sprouting until the time is right. For example, many seeds remain dormant in cold winter months and germinate in the warmth of spring. Some seeds can survive for years, decades or even centuries, before the conditions are right for them to germinate.

▲ When conditions are right, a seed will germinate. A shoot emerges from the seed and grows up to the light. The first root grows out of the seed and down into the soil.

Ancient seeds

The seeds of the Arctic lupin (*Lupinus arcticus*) can survive for an incredibly long time. Arctic soil is very cold and acts like a freezer, preserving things buried in it. It has been reported that Arctic lupin seeds found in a frozen lemming burrow in the Yukon Territory of Canada were 10,000 years old. Scientists managed to germinate some of these ancient seeds within 48 hours!

Nuts

Hundreds of different shrubs and trees produce nuts, but what exactly are they? Nuts are actually kinds of **seeds**. They all have a hard or woody outer layer that forms what we call the shell. Inside the shell is the kernel.

The kernel is the seed and it is also the part that animals, including us, like to eat. Kernels are usually rich in **protein** and **fat** or oil. These are the foods that the seed uses to stay alive. It also uses this food store to grow new **roots** and **shoots**, if it gets the chance to **germinate**. Most seeds need water for germination, but it is especially important for nuts. Nut shells are hard and tough, but water softens them so they break apart more easily to release the seeds inside.

shell   kernel

▲ Have you ever noticed that wild mammals, like squirrels, which eat nuts like these, have strong teeth? They need these to crack open the hard shell.

Top seed

The prize for the biggest nut in the world goes to the coco-de-mer tree (*Lodoicoa maldivica*). Its huge seeds can weigh up to 20 kilograms each but they can float in the sea. The fibres around the shell trap air and the inside of the nut is hollow. The nut floats between islands until it lands somewhere it can germinate.

Nuts on the move

Just like other seeds, nuts are more likely to germinate if they don't have to compete for light, **nutrients** and water with their parent plant. So how do nuts move away from their parents? Before winter, animals like chipmunks and squirrels gather nuts from trees. They eat some, and bury the rest, often in open land. When winter comes and food is scarce, the chipmunk tries to find its food stores. However, just like us, chipmunks are forgetful so they never find all the nuts. These forgotten seeds can grow into new trees in the spring, given the right conditions. If the chipmunk happens to bury the nuts deep enough, they will be protected by the soil until they are ready to germinate!

A hard nut to crack

Brazil nuts, as their name suggests, come from Brazil. In the Amazon **rainforest**, local people pick nuts from wild Brazil nut trees (*Bertholletia excelsa*) in the forest. They have to climb very tall trees to get them. The nuts are hidden inside hard wooden cases, which have to be smashed open. Inside, the seeds are protected in smaller and very hard shells. Brazil nuts often have to hang around a long time before conditions are right for them to germinate!

◄ This hard Brazil nut case has been cut in half to show the white nuts inside their shells.

Cones

Conifer trees do not grow **flowers**, but they still make **seeds**. Conifers have **cones** instead of flowers. Cones are made up of lots of overlapping scales. There are two kinds of cones – male and female. In most conifers both kinds grow on the same tree. When people talk about 'pine cones' they usually mean the female cones and it is the female cones that carry the seeds.

▲ The female cone on this larch tree (*Larix*) is brown and woody. The male cone (at the top) is smaller and softer.

Male cones are smaller and softer than female cones. They produce and release **pollen**, which is usually dispersed (scattered) by the wind. Female **sex cells** are found on the scales of the large female cones. When pollen lands on the female cones it **fertilizes** the female cells and seeds start to form.

Conifer seeds do not have seed coats and so they are called naked seeds. They grow between the scales of the female cones for protection. The female cones thicken, darken and harden as the seeds inside their scales develop and ripen. Some cones, such as Scots pine, change from small and green to large, brown and tough, as the seeds develop.

Kinds of cones

Cones are often smooth and egg-shaped, as on cedar trees, but they can be long and thin, as on spruce. Some cones, such as on the douglas fir or monkey puzzle tree, have prickly scales. Cypress cones are small, knobbly and rounded. The cones of the sugar pine tree (*Pinus lambertiana*), found in the mountains of western USA, can grow as long as 65 cm!

When the time is right

When the seeds are ready, the cones release them. Most cones take a year to mature, although pine cones may take three years. Cones release seeds in two different ways. Some, like pines, open their scales to release the seeds in dry weather. The seeds of Scots pine trees (*Pinus sylvestris*) have a single papery wing that helps them float away from the parent tree. When all the seeds have gone, the cones fall to the ground and gradually rot away.

Other cones, such as those on a cedar tree (*Cedrus*), use a different method. Each cedar scale has two seeds growing on it. When the seeds are ripe, the tip of the cone breaks and gradually the scales fall off. They drop to the ground with the seeds attached. That is why it is rare to see a whole cedar cone fallen from a tree. In some other conifers, the seeds are released as the scales fall.

Fire power!

The Monterey pine (*Pinus radiata*) has cones that refuse to open for anything but the burning heat of a forest fire. The flames destroy other trees, but the Monterey pine is protected by its thick bark. Its cones finally heat up enough to release their seeds, which fall to the ground. As few other trees survive the fire, the seeds do not have to compete for light and **nutrients**, giving them a good chance of **germinating** and growing into new trees.

Spores

Ferns, mosses, liverworts and **algae** are other kinds of plants that do not grow **flowers**, but unlike **conifer** trees, they do not make **seeds** either. These plants **reproduce** in a different way – using spores.

Spores are microscopically tiny flecks of living material. When released from the plant, they are able to grow into a clone – a new plant that is identical to the parent plant. Different kinds of plants produce spores of different sizes and shapes, but most spores consist of a single **cell**. Spores are so small that they are very hard to see, but they are grouped together in packets called **sporangia**. You may have seen sporangia before – on the underside of many fern fronds (**leaves**). They look like dimpled brown pinheads.

Plants release their spores when they are ripe. Spores have a thick outer coat that protects them against harsh conditions and this means they can remain **dormant** for several months or even years until conditions are right for them to develop into new plants. Most moss spores need damp, shady places. Ferns, mosses, algae and horsetails produce millions of spores to ensure that at least some have a chance of landing in conditions right for growth.

▶ The brown spots on the underside of this fern frond are the sporangia that produce the plant's spores. They hold the spores until they are ready to be released.

Spore containers

Different plants produce sporangia that look very different. Mosses and liverworts are the plants that form velvety green carpets over woodland floors, damp walls or riverside tree trunks. In spring, mosses produce **stalks** with a small, oval capsule at the tip. Spores grow inside the capsule.

▲ The capsules on this moss are held shut by a ring of 'teeth'. In dry weather, when the spores are ripe, the teeth will bend back and the spores will be blown away.

Horsetails (*Equisetum*) make their spores in structures that look rather like 'cones'. These grow at the end of tube-like **stems**. The 'cones' of the great horsetail (*Equisetum telmateia*) are several centimetres long on stems around a metre high, surrounded by rings of needle-shaped leaves. Algae make their spores in special places on their fronds. In wakame seaweed (*Undaria pinnatifida*) the sporangia are like little leaves at the base of the frond, but the yellow-brown sporangia of the bladderwrack seaweed (*Fucus vesiculosus*) are at the frond tip.

The sporangia of different **species** of fern have different shapes, too. On bracken (*Pteridium*) they are circular, but on hart's tongue fern (*Phyllitis scolopendrium*) they are like stripes. The sporangia of maidenhair ferns (*Adiantum*) are protected behind little flaps along the edges of the frond.

Stems

Stems come in all shapes and sizes. They range from the flimsy green stem of a primrose to the thick brown and woody trunk of a tree. In a plant like bamboo, the stem is the largest part of the plant. In others, like the cabbage plant, the stem is so short that it appears not to have a stem at all. The stems of many roses are covered in thorns to prevent them being eaten by animals.

Most stems grow up from the ground. Their job is to hold the **leaves** up to the light so that **photosynthesis** can take place and to hold **flowers** in the best position for **pollination**. A stem's other job is to carry water and food to all parts of the plant. It carries these things in tubes. One set of tubes, called the **xylem**, carries water and **nutrients** from the **roots**. Other tubes, called the **phloem**, carry food made in the leaves to the rest of the plant.

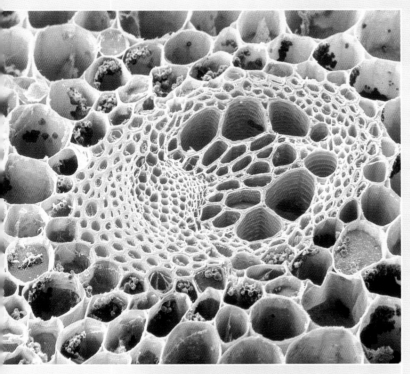

▲ If you look at a cross-section of a stem, like this, you can see the tubes that carry water and food to all parts of the plant.

Going underground

Most stems grow upright, but some grow partly underground, for protection. They may stay underground or grow sideways through the soil. Swollen stems that grow beneath the ground on potato plants are called **tubers**. The potato tuber is the plant's food store – and the part that we eat. On flowering plants such as irises, they are called **rhizomes**.

Water power

Many plant stems are quite hard and firm so that they can stand up straight and support the weight of the leaves and flowers. Most plant stems manage to stand up because they are supported by water pressure. The flow of water through the stem helps them to stay upright. When water is scarce, the stem does not get enough to help it stand tall, and that is why plants wilt or droop.

Going up!

Some plants have weak, floppy stems that cannot support themselves. Runners are horizontal stems that grow across the ground. Strawberry runners produce flowers, leaves and roots at intervals along their length. These form new plants when the runner linking them to the old plant breaks down.

Climbers have floppy stems but they manage to grow upwards. Some, such as morning glory (*Ipomoea*), coil their wiry stems around other plants' stems to help them reach the light. Ivy plants have tiny roots coming out of their stem. These grow into cracks and crevices on walls, anchoring the plant firmly in place.

Some plants, such as pea plants and clematis, send out thin, curly **tendrils**. The tips of tendrils are like long fingers and they are sensitive to touch. They grow out randomly and when they touch something they curl around it.

▼ The stems on a wisteria plant twine around poles or wires to support the plant. Then they become thick or woody.

Trunks and branches

Trunks and branches are the **stems** of a tree. Just like the smaller stems of other plants, their job is to hold up **leaves** and **flowers**. The difference is that the tough, thick stems on trees are made of wood. Trunks need to be extra strong because they have to support heavy branches, twigs and many leaves.

The trunk and branches of a tree are also the places where water, food and **nutrients** move around. Water and nutrients are taken in from the **roots** and sucked up the trunk and along the branches to all the parts of the tree. At the same time, food, made in the leaves, is carried away from the leaves to the rest of the tree. This movement of food and water goes on constantly, just underneath the layer of bark that wraps itself around the outside of the tree like a skin.

The ballooning baobab tree

The trunk of the African baobab tree (*Adansonia digitata*), unlike most other trunks, swells and slims throughout the year. These strange-looking trees, which grow up to 25 metres tall, have very small branches compared to their wide, thick trunks. In the parts of Africa where they grow, there are long dry spells. When a rainy spell comes, the trunk of the baobab tree fattens up with a vast water store. As this store is used up, the trunk of the baobab tree slims down again!

◄ Baobab trees have distinctive, chubby trunks topped with small branches.

Inside a trunk

If you look at the cut surface of a log you will see lots of rings, called **annual rings**, radiating out from the centre. Each ring represents one year's growth. To find out how old a tree is you count the number of annual rings it has in its trunk.

You can also see different kinds or layers of wood inside a trunk. The middle part of the trunk is called heartwood. It is made up of dead, woody **cells** that have become very hard. The heartwood helps to make the tree trunk strong. Closer to the surface is a very thin layer made up of living cells. This is the sapwood, where water and nutrients are carried up through the **xylem** from the roots. It is also where **phloem** tubes carry food made by the leaves to the rest of the tree. The outermost layer is the bark, which protects the sapwood beneath it.

Rubber trees?

Next time you bounce a rubber ball, spare a thought for the tree it came from. Most rubber is made from white latex (**sap**) from rubber trees (*Hevea brasiliensis*). Workers make cuts in the bark and collect the latex that oozes out into cups attached to the tree.

◄ By counting the annual rings on a tree you can tell how many years old it was when it was cut down.

heartwood

sapwood

bark

Bark

Bark is like the skin on your body. It is a tough outer layer that covers the main body of the tree – its trunk and branches – and helps protect the parts inside.

▲ The reddish colour and the curling ends of its outer layer of peeling bark identifies this as a paperbark maple.

Cracking and splitting

Bark does not stretch as skin does. It cracks, splits or peels as a tree grows. Younger trees usually have smooth bark. As the tree grows fatter, the outer layers of bark on the outside split or peel as newer layers inside push outwards.

Different trees have different sorts of bark that can help you identify the tree **species** you are looking at. The bark on a silver birch (*Betula pendula*) is papery, and as its name suggests, is silvery white in colour. The bark of many **coniferous** trees, such as pine trees, flakes off in small, jigsaw-shaped pieces, as the trees grow older. Some trees have distinctive bark patterns, such as the circles on a monkey-puzzle tree (*Araucaria araucana*) or the short stripes on a cherry tree (*Prunus*).

The bark of a tree usually gets thicker as the tree gets older. However, on an ancient beech tree, the bark is thin because older layers flake and drop off. This does not happen to the bark of a redwood tree (*Sequoia sempervirens*), which can be 30 centimetres thick. The redwood's thick bark helps make the tree fire-resistant.

The living dead

We all know that trees are living things, but did you know that apart from the **buds** and leaves the rest of the tree we can see is dead? Bark is made up of two layers. The inner layer that we cannot see is the living, growing part. Every year this special layer of growing **cells** makes a new ring of bark. The new bark pushes the older bark outwards. The old bark is cut off from the nourishing fluids moving through the **xylem** and **phloem** tubes in the tree, and it dies. Then it becomes part of the outer layer of dead bark we can see.

Bark does several very important jobs. It protects the xylem and phloem inside the tree trunk. If bark gets damaged in a ring around a tree trunk, the food and water supply to all other parts of the tree stop and the whole tree can die.

Bark also protects the tree from damage by insects and **fungi**. If woodland animals, such as deer, chew bark, they leave a hole or wound in the tree. If the wound stays open, insects or fungi damage the live wood underneath. Some trees release a sticky liquid (**sap**) from their phloem to plug small holes in their bark. This can dry hard and acts a bit like a sticking plaster.

▶ **Some insects chew softwood, leaving burrows under the bark. If large numbers of insects attack wood in this way, the tree can be damaged.**

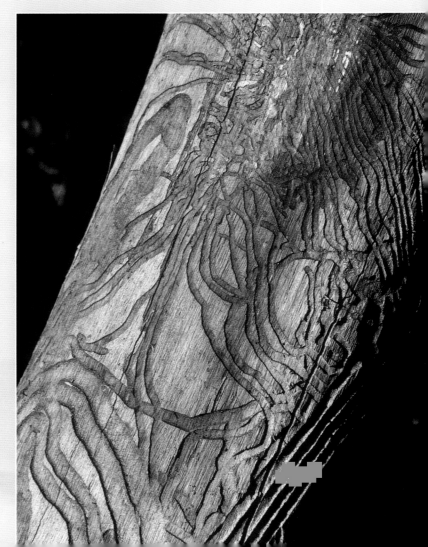

Roots

The **roots** of a plant are like the foundations of a building. Foundations are built underground to hold buildings up and bring in pipes and cables carrying water and electricity. Roots anchor a plant firmly in the soil, holding it in place even in high winds. They also take in water and **nutrients** that are vital for the plant's survival.

Soil secrets

As well as water, people need different kinds of food to stay healthy, such as the **vitamins** found in fruit. Plants need different kinds of nutrients too. They make some foods by **photosynthesis**, but they get other nutrients they need from the soil. Useful minerals come from the very tiny bits of broken-up rock that form part of the soil. Other nutrients come from dead plant and animal matter that has rotted down to become part of the earth.

Kinds of roots

Even though most roots do the same jobs, there are many different kinds, shapes and sizes. The kind of roots a plant has may depend on how large the plant grows and the kind of **habitat** it lives in. For example, plants that grow where water is scarce or the soil is poor grow much deeper roots than other plants, in their search for water or nutrients.

▶ Although it is sad when a giant tree is blown over by a storm, it is a great chance to see how far and wide a tree's roots can spread.

How do roots work?

As a root grows, smaller roots branch out from it. The larger roots are tougher with thicker skins. They help to hold the plant in place. The smallest roots are covered with lots of tiny hairs that have thin skins. These root hairs suck up water and nutrients from the soil. They go into **xylem** tubes in the larger roots and travel up through the **stem** or trunk to the leaves and the rest of the plant.

▲ Even though they may not look it, roots can be very strong. They have to be – they need to be able to push their way through tightly packed and often stony soil. Some roots even have the strength to break buildings or rocks apart. If they grow into cracks in rocks or buildings they can eventually split them apart as they grow wider.

Longest roots

The winner of the record for the longest roots of any plant is the winter rye plant (*Secale cereale*). The winter rye is a kind of grass plant. It can produce over 620 kilometres of tiny roots curled up into a volume of earth the size of a tin can!

Kinds of roots

There are two main kinds of **roots**: fibrous roots and taproots. Plants with many roots, all of which are roughly the same size, are said to have fibrous roots. The many roots spread out in all directions under the ground, but they do not go very deeply into the soil. Plants that have fibrous roots include grasses and many trees. The spread of a tree's roots below ground usually matches the width of its crown (the branches and **leaves** above the trunk).

A plant with a taproot, such as dandelion, has one root that is bigger than all the rest. This main root grows straight down into the soil. Smaller, thinner roots grow out from the side of it. In some plants with taproots, such as carrots or radishes, the taproot becomes swollen with food made by leaves of the plant. This is the part we eat. The plant stores the food like this so it can use it if conditions change and it is unable to make its own food for a while. Some trees, such as oak and pine trees, have taproots.

▶ **This marigold plant grows a main taproot, which is larger than the other roots, which can grow out of it, often sideways.**

Remarkable roots

Special **habitats** require special types of roots. In the Amazon **rainforest**, some types of fig trees are over 40 metres tall, but they grow in shallow soil. To prevent them from toppling over, they have special wedge-shaped roots above the surface of the ground. These buttress roots grow up the side of the trunks and act like feet, helping the tree to stand firm (see right). In Australian **mangrove** swamps, mangrove plants grow in such thick, wet mud that their roots cannot get the air they need. So, they produce some roots that grow upwards out of the water into the air.

Plant parts work together

Each of the plant parts we have looked at in this book is different. The parts look different and they have different jobs to do, but they all work together to form a whole. The roots and leaves supply the plant with the **energy** and **nutrients** it needs. Tubes in these parts and in the **stem** carry water, food and nutrients throughout the plant. These nourish the plant, enabling it to grow and produce other parts, such as **flowers**, **fruits**, **cones** and **spores**. These, in turn, allow the plant to produce **seeds**, which may grow into new plants and the cycle begins again. A plant is a bit like a human body. It may be made up of separate bits, but the individual parts need to work together if the plant is to function – to live, grow and thrive.

Try it yourself!

Try these experiments and activities to find out more about some of the plant processes you have learnt about in this book.

Flower power!

You can make a **flower** any colour you like by using the power in its **stem**.

You will need:

- Two glasses
- Water
- Two white flowers (carnations are ideal)
- Blue and red food colouring (or inks)

Cut 5 cm off the bottom of each of the flower stems. Look at the cut end. Can you see any tubes?

Fill one glass halfway with water and add a few drops of red colouring. Fill the second glass halfway with water and add a few drops of blue colouring.

Stand one flower in each glass. Leave it for a day.

What happens? Your white flowers should change colour. As the stem has taken up water from its base to the flower, it has also taken up the food colouring. The food colouring has dyed the **petals** a different colour.

Bark rubbings

Taking bark rubbings is fun and it is a great way to examine the different kinds of bark patterns trees have.

You will need:

- A pencil
- Brown wax crayons
- Large sheets of paper

Hold a sheet of paper against the bark of a tree. You may need a friend to hold it for you. Rub the crayon lengthways over the paper, not using the point. Try to cover the whole sheet. Write the name of the tree the rubbing came from on the back of the paper with the pencil.

Repeat this process for different kinds of trees.

You could put your rubbings in a scrapbook or make a display of them, with labels telling people which kinds of trees they came from.

Hyacinth happenings

When you grow a hyacinth **bulb** in a glass jar it is easy to see the roots that grow from it.

You will need:

- A hyacinth bulb
- A glass jar with a narrow top (which is about the width of the bulb)
- Water
- Magnifying glass

Fill the jar with water to the point where, when the bulb is sitting on the top of the jar, the bottom of the bulb just touches the water. Stand the bulb in the jar and put them in a warm, light spot, such as a windowsill.

When roots begin to grow from the bulb, take the magnifying glass and look closely at them. You should be able to see the root hairs growing out from the roots.

These root hairs help the roots cover an even wider area as they reach out to collect water for the plant.

If you continue to look after your plant, keeping the water supply topped up, it should produce a colourful, scented flower after a few weeks.

Plant parts we can eat!

Have you ever really thought about which part of a plant you are eating when you munch on **fruit** or vegetables?

You will need:

- A notepad
- Pencil
- Adult to take you to a supermarket

Look at all the different fruits and vegetables in the supermarket and try to identify which part of the plant they are or come from. You could make your findings into a chart. You could use the headings: 'Kind of food', under which you would put entries such as broccoli and celery, and 'Part of plant' under which you would write flower and stem.

Did you also know that you should try to eat five different pieces of fruit or vegetable every day to be really healthy? Which five are your favourites?

Looking at plant parts

Naming plant parts

This diagram of a plant reminds you of the parts that most plants have in common and what those parts do.

Flowers are the plant's **reproductive** part. They make **seeds**, which may grow into new plants, like the parent plant.

Buds hold tiny **leaves** or flowers until the time is right for them to open out.

Fruits protect the seeds as they grow and they help to disperse (spread) the seeds away from the parent plant so the seeds have a better chance of growing.

Seeds are made in the flowers. When they land in a suitable spot they grow into new plants.

Leaves are the food factories of the plant. Leaves collect sunlight, which they use to convert water and **carbon dioxide** into food.

The **stem** holds the other parts of the plant up. It holds the leaves up to collect sunlight and the flowers up so insects or wind can help them disperse their **pollen** and seeds.

Roots anchor the plant in the ground and take in water and **nutrients** through root hairs. Root hairs are usually too tiny to see.

Leaf shapes

Simple leaves

Nasturtium (*Tropaeolum majus*)

Ivy (*Hedera helix*)

Olive (*Osmanthus americanus*)

Pacific dogwood (*Cornus nuttallii*)

Toothed simple leaves

Holly (*Ilex*)

White alder (*Alnus rhombifolia*)

Pussy willow (*Salix discolor*)

Sweet chestnut (*Castanea sativa*)

Simple strap-like leaves

New Zealand flax (*Phormium*)

Tulip (*Tulipa*)

Bamboo (*Arundinaria*)

Iris (*Iris*)

Lobed simple leaves

Sycamore (*Acer pseudoplatanus*)

Sugar maple (*Acer saccharum*)

California scrub oak (*Quercus dumosa*)

Tulip tree (*Liriodendron tulipifera*)

Needles and spines

Scots pine (*Pinus sylvestris*)

Redwood (*Sequoia sempervirens*)

Giant sequoia (*Sequoiadendron giganteum*)

Australian pine (*Casuarina equisetifolia*)

Compound leaves

Ash (*Fraxinus*)

Horse chestnut (*Aesculus*)

Pear tree (*Caragana*)

Coconut palm (*Cocos nucifera*)

Arrangements of flowers

Some plants bear single flowers with one flower at the top of each stem, but most flowers grow in characteristic arrangements. These are listed below with examples for each shape.

Simple flowers

Carnation (*Dianthus*)

Iris (*Iris*)

Oriental poppy (*Papaver*)

Tulip (*Tulipa*)

Buttercup (*Ranunculus*)

Spike

Lots of flowers grow from a stem, each on their own little **stalk**. The oldest flower is at the bottom, the youngest at the top.

Foxglove (*Digitalis*)

Yucca (*Yucca*)

Orchid (*Orchis*)

Pampas grass (*Cortaderia*)

Umbel

Umbels have umbrella-like arrangements of flowers. At the end of a stem are flower stalks of equal length, each with a single flower or tiny group of flowers at the end. The flowers may be held up or down.

Flowering garlic (*Allium*)

Giant hogweed (*Heracleum*)

Angelica (*Angelica*)

Leafy spurge (*Euphorbia esula*)

Composites – flower clusters

This is a slightly confusing arrangement of flowers because it looks like a single flower. In fact the flower head is made of hundreds of tiny flowers packed closely together.

Ox-eye daisy (*Telekia*)

Sunflower (*Helianthus*)

Clover (*Trifolium*)

Edelweiss (*Leontopodium*)

Glossary

algae group of plants that does not have leaves, stems, roots or flowers. We call them plants because they can use sunlight to make their own food in the process of photosynthesis.

annual rings rings you can see when the trunk of a tree is cut down. If you count annual rings, you can find out how old a tree is.

anther swollen tip of a stamen, the male reproductive parts of a flower. Each anther is made up of pollen sacs, which contain grains of pollen.

blade flat part of the leaf

bud swelling on a plant stem of tiny, young, overlapping leaves or petals and other flower parts, ready to burst into bloom

bulb underground bud protected by layers of thick fleshy leaves. An onion is a kind of bulb.

carbon dioxide gas in the air around us that plants use for photosynthesis

carpel name for the female parts of a flower. The ovary, style and stigma together make up a carpel.

cells building blocks of living things, so small they can only be seen with a microscope. Some microbes consist of a single cell, but most plants and animals are made up of millions or billions of cells.

chlorophyll green substance found in plants that is used in photosynthesis. Chlorophyll gives leaves their green colour.

cluster group of flowers growing together

cones form of dry fruit (in which seeds develop) produced by conifer trees. Cones are often egg-shaped and they are made up of loads of overlapping scales in which seeds grow.

conifer/coniferous kind of tree that has cones and needle-like leaves

deciduous trees that lose all their leaves in winter. In cool climates, deciduous trees lose their leaves before winter, but in tropical areas there are deciduous trees that lose their leaves at the start of the dry season.

dormant describes a living thing that is resting before growing

embryo a plant embryo is a very young plant contained in a seed

energy all living things need energy in order to live and grow and do everything – including breathing and eating – that they do

evaporate/evaporation when water turns from liquid into a vapour (a gas). When clothes dry on a line it is because the water evaporates and the vapour becomes part of the air.

fat nutrient that gives living things energy

fertilization when one flower's male sex cell joins with another flower's female sex cell and begins to form a seed

flower reproductive parts of a plant. Flowers contain the parts that can make seeds.

fungi group of living things that are plant-like but do not contain chlorophyll (and are therefore unable to use photosynthesis to make their own food). Toadstools and mushrooms are types of fungi.

germinate/germination when a seed starts to grow

habitat place where plants (and animals) live

inflorescence flower-like head that is made up of lots of tiny flowers (florets) growing closely together

leaves plant parts that make the plant's food

mangrove kind of plant that grows in seashore mud

midrib central vein that runs up through the middle of a leaf

nectar sugary substance plants make to attract insects, which like to eat it

nectary place at the base of flower petals where nectar is made and stored

nutrients chemicals that plants and animals need in order to live

organism living thing, such as a bacterium, cell, plant or animal

ovary part of the flower that contains the female sex cells. It forms the bottom part of the carpel.

petal coloured part of a flower

petiole stalk that attaches a leaf to a stem

phloem tubes that carry food (sugars) made in the leaf to all the other parts of the plant

photosynthesis process by which plants make their own food using water, carbon dioxide (a gas in the air) and energy from sunlight

pod capsule that holds the seeds of legume plants, such as peas

pollen tiny dust-like particles that are produced by the anthers in the male part of a flower

pollinate/pollination when pollen travels from the anthers of one flower to the stigma of the same or a different flower

protein protein is needed by living things for growth, maintenance and repair of their bodies

rainforest kind of forest habitat that exists in very hot and wet (rainy) countries of the world

receptacle swollen end of the flower nearest to the stem

reproduce/reproduction when a living thing produces young like itself

rhizome special kind of stem that grows under the ground instead of up in the air

roots plant parts that anchor plants firmly in the ground and take in water and nutrients

sap sugary liquid containing food made in the leaves. Sap flows in a plant's phloem tubes.

seed the part of a plant that contains the beginnings of a new plant

seed leaves these store food inside a seed. The young plant inside a seed uses the food to provide the energy it needs to grow.

sepal green petal-like structure. Sepals protect the inner parts of a bud until the bud is ready to open.

sex cell special male or female cells that combine to make an embryo. Male sex cells are called sperm, female sex cells are called ovules.

shoot new stem growing from the main stem of a plant, or out of a seed

species kind of living thing. Organisms of the same species can breed together to produce fertile offspring.

sporangia sacs or capsules containing groups of spores

stalk part of the plant that attaches the leaf to the stem. Flower stalks attach little flowers to a stem.

stamen male reproductive part of a flower that produces pollen

stem part of the plant that holds it upright and supports its leaves and flowers

stomata (singular is 'stoma') tiny openings on a leaf, usually on the underside

tendrils very long, thin leaves that wrap around supports to hold up a climbing plant

tuber stem that grows underground and becomes swollen with food that the plant stores inside it. Potatoes are a kind of tuber.

umbel a group of small flowers that form an umbrella-like shape

vein tiny tube that helps support a leaf. Xylem and phloem tubes run through the veins, carrying water to the leaves and foods made in the leaves to other parts of the plant.

vitamins type of nutrient in food that helps animals grow and protects them from illness

xylem tubes in a plant that carry water and nutrients from the roots to all the other parts of the plant

Find out more

Books

Eyewitness Guides: Plant and *Tree*, David Burnie, Dorling Kindersley

Eyewitness Visual Dictionaries: Plants, Deni Brown, 1992, Dorling Kindersley

Internet-linked Library of Science: World of Plants, L. Howell and K. Rogers, 2001, Usborne
www.usborne.com/quicklinks/quicklinks.asp

Magic School Bus: Plants and Seeds, Joanna Cole and Bob Degen, 1999, Econo-clad Books

Plants, Jo Ellen Moore, 1986, Evan-Moor Educational Publishers

The Oxford Children's Encyclopedia of Plants and Animals, 2000, Oxford University Press

The Private Life of Plants, David Attenborough, 1995, BBC Books; also available as a set of videos of the BBC television series of the same name.

Websites

Great Plant Escape: fun way of learning about what different plant parts do; also a simple glossary of terms
www.urbanext.uiuc.edu/gpe/gpe.html

BBCi nature: gardening calendar, fun facts and links to Private Life of Plants information based on TV series presented by Sir David Attenborough
www.bbc.co.uk/nature/plants/

Alien explorer: looks at what plants are like and where they grow, from an outsider's point of view!
www.alienexplorer.com/ecology/topic27.html

Blooming of the titan arum: a website devoted to one of the world's most remarkable flowers – you can see its bud opening!
www.news.wisc.edu/titanarum/index.html

Habitats of the world: at Missouri Botanical Garden's website, you can compare the habitats of the world
mbgnet.mobot.org/index.htm

Conservation sites

Information of dangers to wild plants and habitats and what conservation groups are doing to help them survive

Worldwide Fund for Nature
www.wwf.org.uk

Friends of the Earth
www.foe.co.uk/campaigns/biodiversity

Eden Project: lots of information about the remarkable Eden greenhouses, where different plant habitats have been created, plus an interesting plant quiz
www.edenproject.com

Places to visit

Many museums, arboretums (botanical garden devoted to trees) and botanic gardens are fascinating places to visit. You could try:

The Royal Botanical Gardens, Kew, near London

Westonbirt Arboretum, Gloucestershire

Eden Project, St Austell, Cornwall

You can also find out about plants by visiting local garden centres.

Disclaimer
All the Internet addresses (URLs) given in this book were valid at the time of going to press. However, due to the dynamic nature of the Internet, some addresses may have changed, or sites may have ceased to exist since publication. While the author and publishers regret any inconvenience this may cause readers, no responsibility for any such changes can be accepted by either the author or the publishers.

Index